# A Mother-Father Complex

# A Mother-Father Complex

CARL ANDERSON

Copyright © 2022 by Carl Anderson.

All rights reserved. No part of this book may be reproduced in any form or by any electronic or mechanical means, including information storage and retrieval systems, without permission in writing from the publisher, except by reviewers, who may quote brief passages in a review.

ISBN: 978-1-957384-04-7 (Paperback Edition)
ISBN: 978-1-957384-05-4 (Hardcover Edition)
ISBN: 978-1-957384-03-0 (E-book Edition)

**Book Ordering Information**

Phone Number: 929-334-4203 ext. 1000 or 347-349-4971
Email: info@eamediaandpublishing.com
EA Media and Publishing
www.eamediaandpublishing.com

Printed in the United States of America

# If I Were Her

1.

The dirt in your eyes:
I saw it
and I shut my own eyes
for you not to see
how humiliated I felt
because I didn't want
you to have that victory.

2.

The dirt in your eyes:
I felt it on my skin
and absorbed death
became my nature
and so, you died within me,
since you mirrored your
own hate
on my body.

3.

The dirt in your eyes
was cleverly hidden
by a brain
that deconstructed
every judgement
that came to my mind.
And so I died within you
because from point to point
in our conversations
you moved me
as if I were a wife
from another planet
that I couldn't live on.

4.

The dirt in your eyes
could have been a good dirt
if you had allowed my love
to see the real you.
But you were only words
that moved and moved
and continued to move.
The little justice
I always have given you
could never be steady.
Instead this justice
flew between walls

with my insecurity
led by your scattered mind
so that
I couldn't see
why you exist
for anything else
than for yourself.

5.

My space
was always somebody other's
space
and I felt not the belonging
were we where.
You gave other names to me
than what I am
and I started to think
that others' are myself
without them loving me
and that I can tell you,
you were those names
that should have given love
but instead gave me
a bankruptcy in emotionality
that long nursed
has been in need
not to see you
and not to live with you,
not to see

and not to live a life
with a person
that I certainly
would have been in need
to feel love and affection for

Because so is the world,
we need men that think
and I would have needed your thoughts
many times since we lost each other
if you hadn't been a blank space
for me
that loved others'
than me.

6.

You ate my face
and you ate my tongue
alive.
You swallowed it
squeezed already on my body.
My soul was somewhere
at the tapestries
trying to move out of the apartment,
but then you took my legs
in your hands
and you bent them aside
from each other
with calm and steady grip
over the situation.

As it was I felt a joy
and even a great curiosity.
Then you said something,
-I love you and
my body started to feel
a need to pee,
so I peed on your stomach.
I felt your happiness
when you put your thing into me
but you died soon after
and I felt your desperation
making a sorry for yourself
for not doing better.
You excused yourself
claiming you were high on drugs.
-Fucking drugs-!
-Fucking amateur love maker-!

Don't you see?
Sex is drug forbidden in the
long run
and you had been running
too long to stand up
for love
without escape.

## 7.

I loved you.
I can ascertain you
that I loved you.

I loved you so much
that I completely
from free choice and
without pressure
porn surfed in secrecy
when you were out of
the apartment.
Because I wanted to learn
how to suck cock.
I had before this never seen a porn
and I hadn't even sucked
someone's cock
however much middle age
I am.
But now I learned
how to take care with my teeth
not touching your glans
but to use my lips, my mouth
and my tongue as an open
hot spring.
Then I copied
the women porn stars
and I did
what they are best at
to you.
I did this for you,
because I loved you so.
I was so happy to be with you.

When I was depressed
my lovely mother, that loved you,

always said:
-speak with Anders-,
he will care for you.
It was exciting to be with you
and you had always something
creative to say.
I remember I told you
that I had during my secrete
porn surfing without your knowledge
come across a legendary
male porn star that now is dead,
dead from Aids,
John Holmes
and I described for you
his incredible dick,
so huge,
and I said I felt, yes it felt,
almost ridiculous,
and you said,
-The magnitude of John Holmes
doesn't exists in today's society
without perversion-.
-And John wasn't- you said- a perverse person
or doing any perverse things
but just being a love maker
for the sake of sexual freedom-.
-There isn't place for such men anymore-,
you said.
You were even able to give information
and to be witty at the same time.

I was very impressed by your knowledge

when you said that the male
sexual organ has lessen in size
over a historical period
and that we really don't know
where it will end.
I even remember how
I gave you the lion's kiss
and the mouse's kiss,
and as I now understand,
you stayed with me
for another month
because of the mouse's kiss.
The mouse's kiss is like kittling
a little space on your face
with minimal movements
with the tongue.
I felt we were both small and cute
socially in life,
as I felt our communion
as a space of indigenous love,
not for others' to look at.
We had our secretes
and I was even together and cuddled
with your two little teddy bears
that you liked to have in your hands
when you slept.
Yes, I know,
I even bought one
of them for you

after that your
loved little pink pig
that your mother
had given you before
you got to Dublin

had disappeared from
the room you then rented.
And yes, I know, I was even a bit jealous
with your teddy bears.
Sometimes I felt they meant
more to you than I did.
However, I didn't really understand
your situation in the society
as I do today.
You talked a lot
about influence,
but I didn't really understand
your perception of that.
Today I know you were
in a melting pot
of other people's thoughts
and it might be that I can
forgive the one
that suddenly and without greater notice
left me blind for the deep connection
we had.
This man that you were
that made me so happy
that I did things for
that never would have come

to mind without you
that just in a second
said goodbye,
opened the door
and disappeared from me
like a shadow
from some kind of a spy movie
when suddenly a friend
becomes the worst enemy in my life.

# My Dog Father Shadow and My Pussycat Mother Tongue

1.

Old man sits on a chair,
and his dog dies from a bullet
from a terrorist.

The dog has an open scare
dead for no reasons at all.

Then the dog starts to walk again
and it only stops at its masters
leg, sniffing in the Manchester cotton,
sniffing in old man's smell.

Then the terrorist understood
he is a grandson of the old man

and that he shot the old man's dog
with a stone,
a stone he found on the street
and just randomly picked up
and used because he had until then
not understood he is his grandfather's heir.

The old man forgave

but wasn't happy until
the dog had forgiven,
a forgiving that the dog gave
when the grandson
didn't do the negatively randomly anymore,
or didn't do the negatively routinely
because he is a boy.

The grandson and the dog
became friends
because they really only had each other
after that the grandfather
had become blind.

Grandfather's blindness
made him fell in stairs
and on pavements.
One day he died
over three hundred years old
and the last thing he said

was that "revolutions are a good thing
as long as they don't cut your head off ".

The dog started to bark
and yell
but looked with love on the grandson.
They then ate a meal
with potato from the region
and beef that the dog
had mixed up with eggs, milk, water
some flour, salt and onion.

2.

My pussycat mother tongue
gave a command
and I said no.
She gave me another command
and I still said no.

Follow me
my pussycat mother tongue said
and I said no.

Follow me down the basement
and help me with the cleaning,
my pussycat mother tongue said to me,
and I said no.

You know what we call somebody
like you, my mother tongue pussycat said,
a toddler, or in Swedish,
-du är en unge inte torr bakom öronen-.
You know what that means in English?
-It means you are a toddler
not dry behind your ears-.

I couldn't say then,
but I say it know.
-I have anxieties my
mother tongue pussycat and
sometimes I can't move myself
out of bed.
I just can't and I have a dim light
in front of my eyes
where I hear my pussycats' mother tongue

telling me I can't.

So, I ask myself:
should I do as you say?
or as you intentionally say?
And suddenly you said:
I will follow you
and I will follow you
until I know how we
can be friends.

And I said:
I will walk
and I will walk
until I know who you are.

3.

I gave you a million
for Africa's sake
when you were born,
my dog speaks
in my dreams.
And I gave you
your mother
as a diamond
to hang around your neck,
he whisper,
when I wake up.
I even gave you
my friends
as a testicle
to hold in your hands
when the wind blows
at its most serious level,
he continues.

I know,
I say to myself,
in a lonely apartment.
And you know what,

my dog shadow father,
I was at a café and
I gave the girl whom served me
my satisfaction
and she sent in
a thousand Swedish Kronor
right into my ears
because I was friendly.

She did it with your money
of course,
but she acted it out
even though
it was your money
that paid her
to make me believe
that life isn't a shitty bastard
place to be at
and that is good
and something new to me.

## 4.

But the fact is,
I lost a million
already when
I started to communicate
with friends at my age
early in life.
They told me
I am ugly

and then
my life was over
and your million
was for no use
at all.
And my mother has costed
me a journey
that might have costed me
every jewel
you have hanged around my neck.
Your own friends that you gave me
have been my raw models
but when the wind blew
at its most serious level
they dissolved
as were they Blow bubbles.

5.

It's not the end of the story,
but once I were in England,
sick, humiliated and lost
and you were in Sweden
when you started to count my age
in my mind.
You said:
now you are three years old;
and now you are twenty;
and now you are eighty-eight;
and now you are in childhood again
being two.

-You are in England doing a Master
and you are right now
two years old-.
-Would it not be in time
to believe what I believe in-?
What is that?
I asked my mother tongue pussycat.
That is work – she said and
only for that question are you
twenty-five as you should be.
But I feel me questioned all the time,
I said.
-You hesitate – and you are only four years old
right now-,
my pussycat mother tongue prolonged.
I feel that nobody likes me,
I actually feel me hated,
I said.
-And now your actual age are thirteen,

she continued.
Okay, I get your point,
I shouldn't argue like that.
-And now you are a grown up
being sixty years old
like your father-.
-Stay there, if you can, she said-.
But my father isn't able,
I quarreled.
-Alright, my pussycat mother tongue said,

now you are only one year old
and you are still doing a Master in England,
a Master you won't have success with.
However I have hope for you.
It's just that time isn't right at the moment.
You need to live hundred more years
before the manufacturer
can take your point of view-.

6.

-Write- says my dog father shadow.
Yes, I will I say,
and I go to the computer
and I write
trying to understand myself.
-I give you hundred Swedish Krona
for every idea
you let into your head and out to other people-,
my dog father shadow says to me.

However, I need food, I say,
but I have anxieties to go out
and get me a meal.
I give you ten dollar in pleasures
if you go out and spend
some money
on a tasteful meal,

my dog father shadow points out.
And I do, I go out
and I spend money
on a meal,
and there we go,
I survived it.
It was even a good experience,
I have to remark.

But last night
I drank so terribly much
that I will die
the next upcoming
work week.

I think I overdid it this time,
said in an insecure
mind of regrets.

Each minute with hangover regrets
I will pay you through and through
until you believe,
until you believe
that it's not a crime,
that it's not
a crime to take some pain
for the sake of fun,
my dog father shadow
whispers smoothly in my head.
-And it's not a crime
to celebrate yourself

even if you are alone
in this world-,
he continues.

I feel better right now,
I claim as my bitterness
is losing its grip
over my situation,
speaking with my dog father shadow.

-Write again-,
my dog father shadow asks.
And I write,
I write the negative
and I write the positive.
But sometimes I got anxieties
for the things I write
and then I get to bed

mumbling within myself
wondering if I am completely stupid
who provokes the world as I do.

-Resist-,
I hear my dog father shadow says
as he touches me right on
where it hurts,
right on my soul
so that I can't escape the pain.
But as I stay there,
right on the spot where it hurts
even as it moves
and I follow it
I start to feel a joyful feeling
and it smiles at me,
telling me with the dogs voice
that even if people aren't agreeing
with you,
you will make friends
only if you stay up
for your words.

And the only rule I give you,
my dog father shadow claims,
is not to hate
the people whom aren't
agreeing with you
and you will get
the pleasure
from something
that is for its own sake.

-So, write-,
my dog father shadow says,

because we need to learn
that our thoughts
aren't a heritage
but a communion,

(do you see the point here?
it's not an ownership of things
but a common feeling together)
in its own sake,
a communion
that shares
the negative with the positive
and you know that.
That's why I ask you to write,
he says.

You learned early in life
to take pain from others' pain,
also my pain, he says,
and right now
are your pen
the pain you grew up with,
and it is the only magical thing
you can trust,
my dog father shadow silently whispers.

It's hurtful sometimes,
to think, Sir, I say,
but I am happy I can write
for you, my dog father shadow,
I gesture with my hands
not regretting anything
of all the negations
I have done to my discourse.

## 7.

-Yes, write-,
my pussycat mother tongue
Tells me,

-because then you can see
my negations of you
as a resource
your life never thought of
could be of any use-.

So, please write my words
as if I were
the concrete form
of your ideas,
a cat among other cats
that think otherwise
than what people think
they think.
-And, please, let this
pussycat have fun
so that I don't need
always to feel that life
is just another name
for insolvent hardship-.

# The Silent Girl and the Initiating Father

Look here, says the father,
there is a road
and if you follow it,
it will take you to a store.
Go in there
and look at all the vegetables,
all the yoghurt, all the humus,
the eco potato grown in good soil
without chemicals
and buy the things you need
to be filled with good
and honestly done food.
Then, go home and cock it,
and eat as if every bit,
every spoon full delicacy
make you to a better person.
Eat as if the earths beauty
blends your heart of good belief

with a filled stomach
that doesn't need
to be a spoiled child.

The silent girl looks
with big eyes
and she nods at

the words of the father.
She is thirteen,
she is myself,
she looks at the world
with widespread eyes
and she is silent
and thoughtful.
That is, she is myself,
we share skin and we share
legs, arms and bones,
yes, we even share
the molecules
in our shared body.
But we are not the exact same,
she is a bit different than me
not without hope to take a place
when I am gone,
when I disappear
and nobody knows where I am,
the places only strangers know about.
So, she is a function within me
fully capable of
calling herself

a fully autonomous human.
And that she is.
We are different,
but two examples
of fully autonomous humans
even though we share
our mutual skin, our mutual
legs, arms and bones
and our common molecules,
that make different pictures
about who is who

in this shared body of us.
The father continues to speak.
Look here, he says,
there is a door,
and remember girl,
everything is a door,
but this door is different.
This door is your bathroom door,
he says.
The door into your bathroom
takes you somewhere in mind.
Before you go there, you need to decide
if you go there because of an animal need
or if you go there because
of an uplifting beauty session
with you and the mirror
and the world looking at you
with your own eyes

when you transform
tiredness with color, shade
and grace.
This door means that,
the door into the bathroom
means your animal self
and your beautiful self.
Be careful about who you are
in the moment you are entering it,
the father says.

Look also here, the father says.
Here is a picture of yourself
when you are three years old.
Please keep this picture
as a reference for yourself.

You are different than her
and you will always be different to her,
but when you realize something
she has spoken to you.
This three years old girl child
is my own daughter.
Be kind to her however different
you are to her
and let her enlighten you
when you need to understand
something you haven't understood before.
Because she is my daughter
and I thought her early
to believe in what she thinks

and that can always help you
to be confident
that something is behind
that has been both
a thinker herself
that thinks own thoughts,
but in the same time is my daughter
that I have thought
all the good and the bad
things in life.

The silent girl understood
the father and kept the picture
of herself being three
when she many years later
now sits in an apartment
alone and thinks about her father.
She decides to write him a letter
because they haven't spoken
For many months.
She is still silent when she writes:

Daddy,
thank you for not
having fucked me.
Thank you very much sir
that you didn't fuck me
and split me into two
with you in between.
I am grateful, daddy,

that you never showed your dick
to me
and that you never touched
my pearl between my legs.
I am so thankful to you sir
that you let my little pearl
be only mine
and that you let me decide
who will be in touch
with the self
I like to be when I enjoy.
Thank you sir,
I will always send a thought
of gratefulness
to your capacity
to let me discover things myself
and that you let me discover
this life without a mutilation
in my discerned childhood.

Greetings from your daughter

CPSIA information can be obtained
at www.ICGtesting.com
Printed in the USA
BVHW071751221122
652528BV00006B/328